THRIVING DESPITE THE STORMS
Reflections on the Winter 2023 California Snowstorms

By Southern Trinity JUSD Community
Published by Milestales
Foreword by Ama Karikari-Yawson
Graphic design by Boris Cvekic

Library of Congress Control Number: 2023914381

THRIVING DESPITE THE STORMS

REFLECTIONS ON THE WINTER 2023 CALIFORNIA SNOWSTORMS BY SOUTHERN TRINITY JUSD COMMUNITY

Contents

FOREWORD: RESILIENCE

By Ama Karikari-Yawson

> Life is unpredictable: you never know what joy, pain, frustration,
> or challenge that you will face in the next moment.
> But through it all, you learn who you truly are and what you are truly made of.
> You learn to be resilient.

If there were ever an appropriate word to describe the Southern Trinity Joint Unified School District (JUSD) community, I believe that word would be "resilient."

The past several years have been challenging for the entire globe. The deadly and contagious illness, COVID-19, swept across planet Earth, globally infecting nearly 800 million people and killing over 7 million; in the United States, we lost over 1 million people, and over 100,000 in the state of California alone.[1] Personally, I lost my own mother to the deadly disease in 2021 and I still deeply feel the lack of her love, care, affection, and support.

But, whether individuals lost loved ones to COVID-19 like me or not, we all lost our naiveté. We all lost the belief that such a calamity could never happen. We learned that horror is possible and that we can't take little things—like being able to smile at one another without masks, having a meal at a restaurant together, or sitting in an office or class with others—for granted. Southern Trinity JUSD's first book, *Stronger Than COVID-19*, chronicled the struggles of isolation, loneliness, uncertainty, fear, and frustration during the depths of the pandemic era.

Just when the community thought that they were going to achieve a greater sense of normalcy by beginning the 2020–2021 academic year in person, the community had to postpone re-opening school due to horrific wildfires. In 2020 alone, 8,648 wildfires burned 4,304,378 acres of land in California.[2] But the community pressed on and eventually students were able to return to in-person school. The community was resilient. They bounced back from terrifying misfortune.

Then, shockingly, natural disaster struck again: in 2023, the community saw decades-long snowfall records broken. Trinity County was especially hard hit, and residents struggled through the blizzards to take care of themselves and their animals. Federal, state, and local officials even had to put together an emergency rescue operation called "Operation Hay Drop" to save cattle from starving because the grass was buried under seven feet of snow![3]

In the following book, you will read the reflections of many members of the Southern Trinity JUSD community. You will read about how they dealt with power outages, food shortages, lack of access to medical supplies, at-risk animals, and struggles with transportation. Through their words, we come to appreciate the resilience of the human spirit. It is clear that this community went through a lot, but persevered. They are thriving despite the storms.

---

1   https://covid19.who.int/
    https://www.worldometers.info/coronavirus/country/us/
    https://www.nytimes.com/interactive/2023/us/covid-cases.html
2   https://www.fire.ca.gov/incidents/2020/?ref=goodcover-blog
3   https://www.npr.org/2023/03/13/1163064978/northern-california-snow-storm-cows-helicopter-hay-drop-trinity-county

PREFACE: FIRST TIME FOR MANY

By Peggy Canale, Superintendent, Principal, and Teacher

The snows of early 2023 had a significant impact on our communities and surrounding areas. After many years of below-average rain and snow, being faced with snowfalls of one to two feet at a time with no melt-off in between caught many of us off guard. While there are some in our community, "the old timers," who recall snowfalls like this one, it was very shocking for more recent additions.

I recall looking at pictures of the '64 flood in a photo journal that my grandmother had. I was only three years old when the flood occurred, so I don't remember it. However, I loved to listen to stories my parents and grandparents told about the event later on and the pictures in the book were fascinating to me.

I feel it is important to record these things in order to help us remember and to give us an opportunity to share our experiences with others. It is my hope that readers will enjoy seeing the pictures and reading the narratives, and that it will spark the telling of more stories of how our community faces challenges, works together, and perseveres.

INTRODUCTION: EMERGENCY

By Ama Karikari-Yawson, Editor and Publisher

During February and March of 2023, a winter storm dumped feet upon feet of snow across California, prompting Governor Gavin Newsom to issue a state of emergency in thirteen counties. Many parts of the Golden State were buried under severe snow levels, with some receiving over a hundred inches in one week, according to the National Weather Service. The Office of Emergency Services had to deploy the California National Guard to help dig out snowbound communities in the mountains.

On the following pages, you will read reflections from and see the photos of how these storms impacted members of the Southern Trinity Joint Unified School District (STJUSD) community in Northern California.

THE GREAT STORM OF 2023

Journal Entries By Peggy Canale, Superintendent, Principal, and Teacher

❄ February 22, 2023

Wednesday—Snow started falling today. There were only a few inches in Ruth on the 22nd and 23rd; 2.5" and 1.5", respectively. The power went out in Zenia on the 22nd, but the school's generator worked just fine. We left school early on Thursday the 23rd as the snow was piling up, now at 13". At home that evening, around six o'clock, I suggested to my colleague Principal Andy Felt that we wait until 9:00 p.m. to see if we needed to cancel school. By 7:30 p.m., an additional 3.5" had fallen since I had gotten home—so we decided to cancel school for Friday. I came down with a cold on Thursday night. For that reason, I was glad we were snowed in. I felt pretty slow all weekend.

❄ February 27, 2023

Monday—I started out for school around 6:05 a.m. The road had not been plowed and it was like blizzard, truly white-out conditions! I had to drive in the middle of the road as I could hardly tell where I was. Around Olsen Creek, I received a text from Principal Andy Felt asking if I was on the road. By then it was 6:35 a.m. It had taken me thirty minutes to drive about twelve miles when it usually takes less than half that time. Andy said, "I hate to say it, but we should cancel school today."

I was quick to agree! It took me a good forty-five minutes or more to get back home. My colleague, Tammy, had come over the school section to do her bus run, but the snow was too deep and she could not go back home that way. She passed me around Ruth Lake Community Service District (RLCSD) campground going toward her house via Van Duzen road. She finally got to her house over two hours later!

My trip up our driveway in the truck was a slippery one. As soon as I started up the slope, I was spinning and had to stop near the garden. As I tried to back up, the truck began slipping. There was nothing I could do but hold on. I ended up over the edge of the road with the tail end of the truck just a foot or so away from hitting the pump house. Thankfully, Steve was able to drive it out in low range; no damage to the truck. Whew!

By Peggy Canale, Superintendent, Principal, and Teacher

❄ February 28, 2023

Tuesday—we woke up to 18" of new snow on the deck. Total accumulation: 32"! We haven't seen this type of snow for over thirty years. We had a bit of a break in the weather Wednesday the 1st through Saturday the 4th. This gave us a chance to get our driveway plowed and some roofs shoveled. The power has been on and off all week and seems to be back on everywhere. Maybe we could have school at Van Duzen/Southern Trinity, at least...

By Peggy Canale, Superintendent

❄ March 2, 2023

Thursday afternoon—Jeff England came over with the food bank truck and delivered some food boxes, blankets, and gift cards for some of our families in need. Angie met him at Mad River and helped distribute. Fabio, our county superintendent of schools, has been a great help in checking in with us and reporting our situation to the state. All of our county school districts have been impacted.

Steve and I traveled to Zenia on Friday to check the school and the generator there. The road from Van Duzen Dump to Zenia was virtually one-lane the whole way—lots of snow still on the road and rough! The school driveway had been plowed up to the preschool by Bill Moore with his CAT bulldozer. There was at least three feet of snow on the ground. Plus, the snow from the roof had fallen off, making it almost impossible to enter the building. I was able to get in on one side after hiking through the snow. It was a pretty incredible sight. Unfortunately, Rick and Luke Hall had said they could not get to the school until Monday, at the earliest, to try snow blowing it out. That was before the 16" of new snow fell last night!

Saturday snowfall:
8:34 a.m.   5"
9:06 a.m.   7"
9:45 a.m.   7.75"
11:00 a.m.   9"
Sunday at 7:30 a.m.   17" total, at least 12" of new snow

Of course, the power went out again early Sunday morning around 1:00 a.m., with 16" of new snow today... It feels like we are in a Groundhog Day event. No chance of school tomorrow anywhere with the power out. Maybe Tuesday? I'll keep you posted.
I started taking antibiotics—I need to start feeling better.

By Peggy Canale, Superintendent

❄ March 6, 2023

Monday—Snow flurries, about an inch of accumulation as of 9 a.m.

4:0C p.m.—It has snowed all day, but is not building up on the bare pavement or decks. The mail was delivered! Brit, the mail girl, was able to walk on top of the berm to get the mail in our boxes. The latest power update says we will have power restored at eight tonight.

We have canceled school for tomorrow, as staff are still snowed in at home. Lyndsey and Susan, can't get out. Andy was waiting for Jay to plow him out again. I am not sure about valley folks. Shane said he is still stuck. He was pretty tired from last week's snow dump, and I am sure not excited to leave home any time soon! He also took a tumble on the ice—hopefu ly no lasting ill effects from that. Donna Hall just called me a bit ago and said they got Zenia school cleaned out. I am hoping to travel over there tomorrow to check on things. Maybe school on Wednesday? We will see.

By Peggy Canale, Superintendent

❄ March 7, 2023

Tuesday—5" of new snow on the railing at 6:30 a.m. It snowed all day with little accumulation on the bare spots. The snowy areas get deeper and deeper. The power came on just before noon, as one of the reports indicated. Yay for that! My sister, Diane, was happy because they have no hot water when the power is out. Caitlin and Eric were able to drive down their hill and check on things upriver. However, going back up the hill was out of the question. They parked the pickup up here by the garage and Steve shuttled them up to their house in the buggy.

I asked Cody to go up to the school to see how the snow removal looked for us. He took a video, and is it ever amazing! They did blow the snow away from each door and plowed around the driveway. However, snow was already waiting to fall in the "cave" entrances! Some snow has fallen in against the door—what a sight.

You have to feel bad for the wildlife and cattle. They have nowhere to go to escape the snow, very little feed, and it's hard to get to water too. People have been posting on FB that the quail are huddled next to garages, etc., trying to find a dry space and maybe a seed or two.

By Peggy Canale, Superintendent

❄ March 8, 2023

Wednesday—I kept waking up around midnight and beyond and could hear the snow falling. I got up at 1:15 a.m. to check things out. The railing had 15.5" of snow on it! There were only 5" when I went to bed! It was snowing steadily. As I lay in bed, boom! The power was out again. Steve had to hike out at 1:35 to turn off the generator again. No need to let it run all night. California Safety called me shortly after that and confirmed the school also lost power. The PG&E app says restoration is scheduled for March 9th at 10 p.m.

You should see our house. The snow on the deck has piled up to meet the snow on the railing. There is a huge mushroom-like hump in the corner by the grape arbor. Steve just measured 45" of snow on the deck! That means there is easily four feet of snow throughout our area.

Steve and I traveled to the Fire Hall yesterday afternoon to meet the food bank truck. We loaded up, and Christian Soria loaded up his rig, then we took supplies to VD for distribution tomorrow. Thankfully Angie, Kelsey, and Tamara will distribute in the morning.

Tori took a hike up the hill this evening and brought home a deer head! Yuck! I threw it on top of the garage roof so she couldn't get it. Who knows if a mountain lion killed it, or if it just died from hunger. Steve shoveled one side of the garage roof most of the day—but he is coming down with my cold...

By Peggy Canale, Superintendent

❄ March 9, 2023

Thursday—There was a slight reprieve through the night last night. No snowfall or rain. Snow beginning again around 10 a.m. Caitlin called to say that Susan Gordon's skylights in her garage shattered! I called her. She has it figured out to collect water, etc. So thankful it wasn't her house!

Cody came over, and he and Steve are shoveling more of the garage. This is a big help, as Steve worked for hours yesterday and got about one half of one side done. Steve is still starting to get the cold that I had for almost two weeks. I finally took some antibiotics and feel like I am over it.

11:30 a.m.—snow showers turning to rain....

OES has declared emergencies across numerous counties, but not Trinity! I am trying to contact people to see why we aren't on the list. Southern Trinity should definitely be on it. Angie, Kelsey, and Tamara just handed out food and supplies to forty-three people in Mad River/Dinsmore area! There are some folks who are snowed in that need supplies and can't get out to get them. More evidence of emergency status. Through FB, some are saying it is the sheriff who declares emergency status. I emailed Philip Simi from OES, Dan Frasier, our supervisor, and Tim Saxon, the sheriff, asking them why we aren't declared an emergency.

The other day, Caitlin and Eric shared that Dolly from Ruth Store ran out of propane. Propane runs the generator for the store, which allows folks to pump gas. The propane company said they would not deliver until next week. So, people in Ruth have no way of getting gas or propane if they run out! Jeff England said OES is aware and they are trying to get another company to deliver...I feel for the folks who rely on five-gallon tanks, etc.

Power back on at 4:30 p.m.! There were 2.15" of rain when I went to bed at eleven. As the evening progressed, folks on the Weaverville side of the mountain started getting the snow, wind, and power outages. Join the club! Steve definitely has my cold...

By Peggy Canale, Superintendent

❄ March 10, 2023

Friday—This morning we still have power, and there is currently no rain falling...

Steve measured 3.2" of rain for yesterday. There's been a break in the weather and it's so nice to see blue sky today. Friesen folks from town came out and helped shovel snow from trailers they have sold, as well as other people's trailers. They had a snowcat plow, and we opened the gate for them to go down to Albertini's. Dennis Bermers found out and asked Steve to ask them to do his trailer, which they did. They were very tired from all the trailers they shoveled.

Eric and Caitlin have been waiting for Lin Dillon to come plow Terral Road so they can get back up to their house once they come down. He finally showed up around 3 p.m. He plowed up to Peter's and will come back to finish tomorrow. Highway 36 was closed part of the day due to an avalanche a few miles west of Forest Glenn!

By Peggy Canale, Superintendent

❄ March 11, 2023

Saturday—Steve and I went to Eureka and Fortuna to get groceries. We were going to go to Redding, but changed our minds as it is so uncertain what the roads would be like from South Fork through Dubakella. We got our groceries and stopped to see Doris for a few minutes. Cody sent some pictures of the school at HZ—it is literally buried! Rick Hall said he would go there first thing tomorrow to plow again. We are going to go over tomorrow and hopefully get ready for school Monday. We have missed 11 straight days of school! Today was showering off and on. Some snow is melting, but also soaking into the snow. It's going to be a slushy mess.

I do want to commend our county road crew. There are just four of them. I think they have done a tremendous job clearing the roads, especially considering their small crew and limited equipment. I'll bet they are exhausted. I just got a brainstorm to make a pictorial documentary book of this weather event. While not nearly as awesome as the '64 flood, it is still the biggest storm many people around here have ever seen. I hope I can get folks, students, and teachers to contribute.

By Peggy Canale, Superintendent

❄ March 12, 2023

Sunday—No church as the snow is over the heater vent, which causes the exhaust to enter the building. Pastor Todd didn't feel it was safe. That was OK with me as I needed to go to Zenia and see how things are. The road over is plowed down to pavement, but much of it is only one lane. I hope I don't meet anyone tomorrow. We did meet one truck, but thankfully it was a wider area of the road. Rick Hall had just finished removing the snow with his snowblower. It kept getting plugged with the wet snow. Steve and Cody shoveled snow away from the doors for me. There is still some on the roof that will probably fall in the way, but at least now it's manageable.

The rain is falling and folks are getting worried about flooding. Steve measured an inch this morning, and we definitely are getting more today. The cell service went out yesterday afternoon. I emailed OES and Fabio to hopefully get them to move on it soon. Others have contacted Verizon too. I do hope we don't have to wait months to get service back like we did after the August Complex.

I posted my idea for a storm book and got two responses: Tammy sent me pictures and a narrative, and another guy indicated interest because he is writing a blog. I am excited and hope many people will join. I am going to make my students do it, so at least we will have that many narratives!

By Peggy Canale, Superintendent

❄ March 13, 2023

Monday—We are back to school after eleven days of being out due to snow, power outages, or just staff and students' inability to reach the road to travel to the different schools. My drive to Zenia is like going through a tunnel in many spots. I crept around corners on the one-way lane to avoid a collision. I guess it's a good thing I leave home in the dark, as I can at least see headlights coming and can pull over as-needed. There are few people on the road at this time of the morning, so I avoided any close calls.

By Peggy Canale, Superintendent

❄ March 25, 2023

Saturday—As the snow has melted, the county has been able to push the berm over to make a two-lane road again. But the number of cracks and drop-offs in the pavement are incredible. The crack at Bar Creek seems to be growing by the day, and I fear the road to Zenia is going to become impassable soon. There is also a big drop-off between our home and Ruth Recreation Campground. It has dropped over a foot in the past week. I am anxious about the roads, especially since the school section has been closed and I am having to drive around through Van Duzen to get to Zenia. Many of us have contacted the County Road Dept. Director, Panos Kokkas, regarding when they will be able to begin repairs. Of course, there are a multitude of hoops to jump through. He has indicated it could be years before all the paperwork is done and approved. Ugh!

By Peggy Canale, Superintendent

❄ March 28, 2023

Tuesday—I've been looking at the weather app on my phone and it has been saying for over a week that we would get major snow today—up to 22"! Steve scoffed at this, which is reasonable, as the weather predictions can change drastically in a day let alone a week. It started to rain last night, and although the app said it would begin snowing around 6 p.m., it mostly rained with only a mix of snow all through the night.

Steve measured 1.32" of rain this morning. The roads were slushy and a mess. Tammy and Rolinda head out first thing on their bus runs, and I got word at six that the roads were extremely slippery and it wasn't safe to be out and about. So, another canceled school day. Snow started around eight and is falling steadily now. I have a strange feeling we are going to have even more pictures for our book!

By Peggy Canale, Superintendent

❄ March 29, 2023

Wednesday—There was about 4" of snow at the house when I left for work. Shane texted and said he got about 8" at his house in Hettenshaw. Because we start so early, the road has only been plowed from Jonathan's house. I met Tammy on the road and she confirmed that everything was still unplowed the rest of the way. I tried to make my own tracks most of the way to school because it was very slippery in the tracks from other vehicles.

Two hours later, I finally arrived at the school driveway. I thought the truck would make it up in low gear—but I promptly started spinning and then was stuck. I hiked up the hill to the school, and it looks just like it did several weeks ago: We are again in a snow tunnel with barely any way to get in or out of the building. When I measured the buildup here, there were 13–16"!

No wonder the truck couldn't make it! Cody came up yesterday and made tracks around the driveway, but it wasn't enough for us to make it up this morning.

Thankfully, Cody also came today and got me unstuck and turned around. It's now time for the slow trip home...

This most recent snowstorm experience was definitely an interesting one. It is sad that so many people were unprepared for bad weather. Many folks were very low on food, and just as many ran out of wood for their fireplaces.

But, as usual, we all persevered and came through with minor issues. Many people's kindness was exhibited throughout our area as folks like Jay and Lin Dillon plowed driveways to allow people to get to the county road. They did so on a donation basis only, so no one was left out. Other community members shoveled roofs for whoever needed it. The Friesen family from Fortuna—who were also very helpful during the August Complex by building and providing storage sheds for people who lost their homes—also made the trip out to Ruth to shovel roofs. All this is very heartwarming.

By Peggy Canale, Superintendent

BURIED

Photos Submitted By Various Community Members

These striking images reveal the storm's severity and show people's attempts to dig themselves out.

#1 Cabin Before Shoveling

#2 Cabin After Shoveling

Uncovering 2,500 gallon water tank

An RV towards the top of Bell Springs Road is partially covered in snow. [Photo by Virgil Scigla]

'SEND HELP IF YOU CAN': RURAL RESIDENTS TRAPPED BY SNOW FOR NEARLY TWO WEEKS STRUGGLING TO SURVIVED

By Matt LaFever, Mendocino County Educator and Journalist with Kym Kemp, Journalist, Photographer, and Entrepreneur

These striking images reveal the storm's severity and show people's attempts to dig themselves out.

An unusually harsh winter dumped snow on the rural mountains of northwestern California nearly two weeks ago, stranding residents and leaving some with dwindling to nonexistent supplies. Humboldt County's Second District Supervisor Michelle Bushnell says the snow hasn't been this deep since 1989 and, this time with snow falling clear to sea level at times, ranchers and other rural dwellers are unable to get out to resupply.

The Hoaglin-Zenia School inundated with snow. [Photo from Peggy Canale]

Many of these folks are used to snow and having to hunker down for a week without resupplying, but the latest rounds of snow pushed them to their limits.

Bushnell told us, "Some have snowdrifts to top of their houses. It's not manageable."

Some have medical needs including medicine that is running out or is already gone. Others are out of fuel and food for themselves and their animals while ranchers are struggling to feed their livestock. Water lines have frozen leaving residents and cattle without an easy way to quench their thirst.

Today, we received a letter from a man who lives east of Laytonville in Mendocino County.

Good morning Kym,

I've been stuck on Iron Peak for 12 days now.

There's 3' of new snow since last night and it's still dumping at 6a.m. With all the talk in the news about folks being rescued in So Cal but nothing about Mendocino county. Is the issue being addressed by anyone in authority?

I'm out of some of my meds, running low on food and am starting to get worried… I've called the California OES, and the Mendocino county sheriff and was told there was nothing they could do until the governor includes Mendocino county in the most recent declaration. And then there's not much they can do because Mendocino county doesn't have the equipment to remove so much snow.
There's about 10 people on my road in worse condition than me, I have power, water, heat, a working phone. One guy has been sitting in a 5th wheel in the dark, no gas, propane with 2 dogs. He ran out of gas and propane 4 days ago. The snow is too deep to check on him, and there's others who are in different states of desperation up here. Send help if you can. I'm beginning to fear for peoples lives.

Have a warm dry day,
Deano [Criscitiello]*

This morning, Humboldt County Second District Supervisor Michelle Bushnell spoke to us from her rural ranch in the southeastern part of the county. "I'm trying to dig out right now," she explained.

But, she said, This is "500 times worse than a normal winter. In 1989 was the last time it snowed this much. And this time snow went to sea level which didn't happen in 1989. So there is nowhere for stock to get down to some grass."

The snow keeps falling. "Last night, an additional foot fell," she told us. In places, she said, "The snow is deeper than the calves are tall."

Ranchers are having to buy feed and haul it to where their livestock are but…the snow is making that impossible in many cases, she told us.

When the snow fell hard in late February, it came in wet and heavy breaking multiple trees and pulling down power lines and even poles. The downed trees not only blocked main roads and county roads but trapped some residents behind a jumble of broken branches

Calf in the snow. [Photo provided by Supervisor Michelle Bushnell]

and thick trunks which crisscrossed their private driveways.

Since then the snow has stopped for only a day or two but then continued. Residents are running out of fuel to run ATVs and chainsaws and even to run their own homes.

Bushnell told us that county staff, the CHP, County road workers, local volunteer firefighters, the Sheriff's departments, PG&E, and neighbors are exhausted as they struggle to help everyone.

"We don't have [snow like this]," Bushnell explained. "We're not used to it and we're not prepared for it...Shoveling snow out is exhausting and it keeps coming." She described the process of clearing roads of snow and then having snow fall again as "the ultimate groundhog day."

Mendocino County Supervisor John Haschak is aware of at least two rural residents socked in by snow and low on provisions, one in Bells Springs and the other on Spy Rock Road. From reports he has received, those folks are being supported by neighbors till the weather clears.

Laytonville radio station KPHT DJ Long John recounted his experience of being rescued by Mendocino County Search and Rescue team. He had been socked in by snow since February 21, 2023 stuck at the top of Bell Springs Road. The snow quickly piled up and John realized "there was no way I could get out to resupply meds and propane."

He ran out of meds, had but a "whisper of propane", and a friend of his contacted Mendocino County authorities. Next thing he knew, MCSO called John and said help was on the way.

A cow eats from a protein bucket on a rural ranch in Southern Humboldt County. "The cows are camped on them right now," Supervisor Michelle Bushnell told us. [Photo from Supervisor Bushnell]

He sat and waited and finally heard the sound of a motor coming down his driveway. Outside, a group of men on a SAR ATV fitted with tracks were there to take him to safety.

John rode with the men down the mountain while the Laytonville Fire Chief went to a pharmacy to get his heart medication. Since then, he has been in a Willits motel, "warm and dry" thankful to all those that "came through in a BIG way and I'm now safe from a bad outcome."

Communities are trying to rally. On Thomas Road west of Miranda in Southern Humboldt County, locals hired heavy equipment operators to clear their main road and individual landowners paid for their driveways to be cleared. On Alderpoint, volunteers assisted county workers when the snow was too deep for county vehicles.

But, the need is great. Bushnell said she talked to 22 ranchers yesterday. "Only one said we got it," she told us. Most, she said are struggling and telling her, "We have cows stuck and we can't get to them."

Bushnell told us there is hope-a coordinated operation involving the Coast Guard, Cal Fire, and the Humboldt County Sheriff's Department are dropping hay to remote ranches by helicopter to feed starving livestock. Operation John Wayne (the name an attempt to bring a little humor during rough times) is commencing today.

Humboldt County Supervisors Michelle Bushnell and Rex Bohn reached out on behalf of not only their constituents but the surrounding countys' residents. Because in an emergency county borders don't matter to the people and animals needing help, Bushnell told us Operation John Wayne is "not specific to Humboldt–they are flying to Trinity and Mendocino" as well.

"Diana Totten is the person to call," Bushnell explained that the experienced Southern Humboldt leader is in charge of gathering coordinates from ranchers who need to get food to their livestock. Her number is (707) 223-2455. "Our first drop's today," she told us. The hay will be dropped into Rainbow Ridge out by Scotia. The drops are structured by need–how many animals and how long have they been without food.

And, there is help available to rural residents of Humboldt County. Bushnell explained, "If you are stuck and you need help, I have a number for you–(707) 445-7251. That's the Sheriff's Department." She explained that they are able to send in their Snowcat. "They'll get to you if you need medicine or out of food or heat," she said. But please don't call unless it is necessary so that the equipment can be used for those that need it most. She also suggested that as snow is supposed to last through Wednesday, "if you get out, try to go to a place where you won't be stranded again."

Mendocino County Sheriff's Office Matt Kendall told us his agency will deploy search and rescue personnel for anyone running low on food, fuel, or other provisions. But, those residents will evacuate with his personnel.

He told us he has received calls from residents requesting supplies be delivered, which he said his agency will not do. "We are no DoorDash. I am not going to ask search and rescue to go out and deliver Snickers bars. We will deploy if someone cannot survive, but we're going to take you into town and shelter you."

County crews plow roads made accessible by dozer operator [Photo by Shanon Taliaferro]

Humboldt County Supervisor Michelle Bushnell urged neighbors to think who they can check on and assist. "Don't wait to be asked," she said. "If you think you can help, please do that."

She noted that after Wednesday, the weather is predicted to warm up and rain is coming "which can cause its own set of problems." With thoughts of how the heavy snow of 1964 was melted by warm rain and caused an unprecedented flood, she pointed out, "[The coming warmer weather] is making everyone nervous."

Bushnell urged everyone to remember that this is a crisis. "Please don't beat up on anybody right now," she asked. "Wait till afterward and we can use [what happened] as a learning experience. Some folks have never been through this type of snow." The closest similar snowfall happened over 30 years ago–an entire generation of people living in the hills have never dealt with this type of emergency situation and are not prepared.

But Bushnell said when a crisis happens in Humboldt County, "We come together in disasters and we've proven it over and over again."

*After sending the email, Deano Criscitiello learned that a local equipment operator will be able to help. "He's going to start plowing again tomorrow morning," Criscitiello told us.

BIG SNOW OF 2023

By Dottie Simmons, Community Member

It started snowing February 22nd, and snowed through March 8th with only a short break. It's been a decade since we've seen such a series of low-elevation snow storms—maybe longer. While it does provide day after day of unimaginable beauty, a big snowstorm is also full of hardship.

Thankfully, we are well set to hunker down and roll with a big storm. We have seen them before and pay attention to what must be done alongside being aware of what we must try not to do, especially as we seem to have grown older over the years (fancy that!). We try to always have food and firewood on hand as if the winter will be a hard one—and, as this year shows, sometimes it is. We try to have extra supplies of animal feed and fuel for the generator, in case we need back up for our power system, like we did this time around too.

So much is entailed in a storm like this: from clearing paths, to tending our animals, to bringing in firewood, to dealing with power outages or perhaps frozen pipes. Being prepared is key for any level of security. In our case, clearing our solar panels had to wait until there was enough of a break that we felt they wouldn't immediately get covered up again. When we finally got to get out and do it, our pleasure at that exhausting job (wet snow is heavy) was deeply dampened by finding a perfect yearling deer curled, as if sleeping, likely frozen to death, beneath our panels where deer often take shelter in storms. It is heartbreaking. My heart is heavy, for I know that this one deer is likely only one of many hunkered down, frozen, and starved under trees on the mountain. This happened back in 1989 as well.

It's easier to help the humans who are in trouble. We know where they are and can move resources to come to their aid. But, we humans are not the only ones who suffer. We did what we could helping people connect to resources (since we couldn't get out ourselves to help), and for the wild birds we put grain in places they can get to. But we had nothing here available to put out for the deer this time, which breaks our hearts.
We moved the little deer to a place where the turkey vultures, who are also suffering in this storm, could find it.

But then, on this selfsame sad day, we see one of the CalFire helicopters low and searching for cattle on the ranch across the river from us. We watched them drop bales of hay for the cattle, and it's likely some will be shared by the wildlife as well. This is a wonderful sight. It's an example of people and organizations and government working together in difficult times to help one another in the best of ways. This is one of those times: a record-breaking storm that will go down in history for all its beauty and wonder and hardship. We will be telling stories about it for years to come.

ROADS RAVAGED

Photos Submitted By Various Community Members

The following photos were submitted by community members, and demonstrate the terrible impact the snow storm had on roads. Repeated melting and refreezing of snow enables it to seep down into small cracks, which eventually grow very large—creating a dangerous situation for motorists.

BROUGHT DOWN IN THE BLINK OF AN EYE

By Pam Peace, Community Member

The 27" of snow that I got here overnight proved to be too much for the poorly-constructed roof over my porch and my already-compromised woodshed. The failing beams prevented me from being able to get on the roofs to clear them safely.

I was bringing the wood out on the porch into the house when my little rescue dog, Harry Potter, started barking at me. I got him to quiet down, then could hear what he was trying to warn me about. Pop, pop, pop—the bolts holding the porch roof up were pulling out of the wall!

I could see the doggie door shifting in the frame and the sliding glass door bowing in towards the house! And my old, can't-hear-well dog was laying in front of it!

I got the animals and myself out of there and around the corner to a safe spot, where I pulled out my phone to record the demolition. But before I could put my finger on the camera button, the roofs were already on the ground! What I'd planned on spending spring taking apart, Mother Nature brought down in the blink of an eye.

As I look at the massive clean-up job ahead of me, I can't help but shed a tear to think that I was just under there—and that the little dog whose life I saved before had probably just saved mine.

SNOW DAYS

Journal Entries by Terri Willburn, Assistant at Hoaglin-Zenia Elementary

❄ February 23, 2023

It started to snow on the evening of the 22nd. This morning, there was about 10" of buildup, but I was able to get to school with all of the kids. Because it was snowing so hard, we went home early. Mrs. Canale said that we would know by six if there would be school on Friday.

❄ February 24, 2023

I got up at the normal time and got ready to go to school. When I looked outside, I noticed that there was about 18" of new snow: not a good thing. My sister, Tammy, called to say the roads were bad and to be careful—it had taken Mike twenty-five minutes to get to the break in the road where she got the suburban.

I got a text that school was canceled just before it was time for me to leave, and let Tammy know. She wasn't happy. It took her two hours to get back home. She was right, the roads were bad! I went out and shoveled to my almost-empty woodshed and refilled my wood box. I praise God that we still have electricity!

By Terri Willburn

❄ February 25, 2023

Seth and Jarrett both plow my driveway. Yah! The difference is that Seth plows with a side by side and Jarrett plows with a CAT bulldozer. Seth missed the real driveway, but it's still a way out. Jarrett brought a skidder down to move snow, but it has no lights so he just parked it in my driveway.

By Terri Willburn

❄ February 26, 2023

Sunshine in the morning. Yah! Dan borrowed the skidder and plowed a path to the woodshed, and to Mom's house so they could get the wood. Then Dan, Kendall, and all of the kids brought me four loads of wood, thank God! Ridge climbed through all of that snow to check my water and got it running again. I made a pot of chili as a thank you for the wood. Wow, I have wood and water—so awesome. And to top it all off, we still have electricity.

By Terri Willburn

❄ February 27, 2023

It snowed again last night: another 10". This has gotten really old and the weather app said more is coming, dang. School is canceled again, but I have wood, water, and electricity, so I'm good. I shoveled to the woodshed too. Thank God they plowed in front of the house so I didn't have to shovel that as well.

By Terri Willburn

❄ February 28, 2023

More snow, so much snow. The power went out overnight, wahhhh. I hate snow! All I can see is white humps instead of cars or the gas tank. I'm hiding in my house today. No water again. In this case, I'm glad for the snow, so I can melt it for water.

By Terri Willburn

❄ March 1, 2023

Still snowing and more shoveling! I hate snow! Jarrett brought the CAT bulldozer through again and cleaned out the driveway. Seth had been plowing multiple times a day, but he broke something on the side by side. Darn.

By Terri Willburn

❄ March 2, 2023

Even more snow and shoveling! Jarrett had to walk down through the snow—three feet of the crap—to borrow five gallons of gas and come back home with it because Cadence got the four-wheeler stuck while going to feed the pigs and dogs in the upper valley.

By Terri Willburn

❄ March 3, 2023

More snow in the morning, but we had a break in the afternoon. Jarrett brought the CAT bulldozer through again while Tammy and I were shoveling out the car and the suburban. He told us if we got the car out, he'd plow the suburban out for us. So cool!

We also got the generator shoveled out and started! Yah! I finally got to charge my fridge and freezer. The amazing thing is that even my ice cream hadn't thawed. Shane brought the school pickup with a plow on it and cleared my driveway before Jarrett got back with the skidder.

Shane got stuck and pulled the suburban out of its hole—and broke the front of it—so I could pull him out. He finished plowing around my yard and plowed to the main road. Then it started to snow again. This has gotten really old! The power came back on an hour after we got the generator started.

By Terri Willburn

❄ March 4, 2023

PG&E called at 12:18 a.m. to tell me the power was out. I got an adrenaline boost and couldn't go back to sleep until five. It's still snowing, and so far there is another 10". I shoveled to the woodshed again and filled the wood box. I'm so glad I moved the cars out. We also had a short break in the storm.

By Terri Willburn

❄ March 5, 2023

Jarrett plowed again. I don't know why, it's not like I can get out anyway. The county hasn't been through the valley in days. More snow—a foot this time. All of the shoveling I did yesterday was totally erased! Crap!

By Terri Willburn

❄ March 6, 2023

More snow! I was out shoveling again to get to the woodshed and the generator, whining to God about the snow, when a small voice in my head said, "This is what you prayed for." I thought, "Crap, I did!" so no more whining. We had a little blue sky for a while and then snowing again. Still no water, but we have electricity. Yah! This time, I vacuumed.

By Terri Willburn

❄ March 7, 2023

Wow! Sunshine and blue sky! Oh my eyes, it's so bright after days of nothing but gray skies. We got 18" of snow last night, so I shoveled early and got my wood inside. The weather service is calling for more snow, again.

By Terri Willburn

❄ March 8, 2023

More snow, more shoveling. Jarrett was going to go to town today, but he was snowed in. He should have listened to me, lol. He went to get the CATbulldozer again. This time, he plowed Mom's driveway and then went to the water tank and plowed down the hill. Then, he plowed to his house and up to his pigs.

By Terri Willburn

❄ March 9, 2023

Susie and I drove up to the water tank in her side by side, then shoveled for an hour and a half to get to the tank—only to find that the water coming in was frozen. Crap! It made us both want to cry. While we were shoveling, Jarrett headed for town to get groceries and feed for the stock. So, back to the house to whine and pout.

Later, Susie took me to Tammy's for a shower, and it felt so nice. That was the first time I'd been away from my house since the storm started. We had to hang our heads out of the side by side because the snow kept covering the windshield.

Mike went to Dinsmore, and when he got back he told us the roads were awful. It had started to rain and made everything mush! Yuck. I called Jarrett and told him. Not good. He said as soon as his hay was loaded, he'd head home. He texted at 8:06 to say if he wasn't home by 9:30, come find him.

He got stuck on the bridge at the end of the valley and Mike went to save him. They couldn't get it unstuck, so they left it in the middle of the road and came home. What a long, disappointing day! The snow slid off the back roof at 11:30 and scared the crap out of me. I thought it had broken my bedroom window. It hadn't, but it woke me up with a start and it took a while to go back to sleep.

By Terri Willburn

❄ March 10, 2023

Jarrett took the skidder down the valley, plowing all the way to the car. It took him three hours to get the car back to my house. He had all of my groceries, water, and gas. Yah. It's still raining. The National Guard dropped hay to the cows. They sounded a siren before they dropped it, so they had to chase the cows back to the hay after. It was almost dark before Jarrett got the hay into Angel's barn. All was well—we both had drinking water and gas.

By Terri Willburn

❄ March 11, 2023

It's still raining. I can see out my front window, and light at least comes through a little. I no longer live in a cave! I started shoveling the suburban out and made it an hour and a half before I was pooped out. I only got about a quarter of it shoveled, but a man came with a backhoe and cleared most of the rest! Yahoo! What a blessing! I only had about a half-hour left to shovel before I could just pull the car out.

By Terri Willburn

❄ March 12, 2023

I pulled the suburban out and cleaned it off. Then, I parked it by the house to be ready for school tomorrow! It's still raining and I can hear the creek roaring from my house; it's really rolling along.

By Terri Willburn

FURRY AND FEATHERED FRIENDS

Photos Submitted By Various Community Members

The following photos submitted by community members show that human beings were not the only ones at risk due to severe weather. Animals certainly had to contend with the elements, too.

SNOWED IN, BAD...

By Jesse Ragsdale, Community Member

Since February 22nd, we've been getting pounded by multiple heavy snowstorms. Shoveling snow daily is the norm. At times, there has to be a minimum of four shoveling sessions a day! I've been working all the muscle groups harder and harder. I've lost yet another pant size, and those size 34s that used to be just a little snug are now super loose. I seem to be maintaining a weight range of 167–175 these days. It's a good workout, yes, but holy hell is this killing me...

There have been multiple power outages, the longest being two and a half days. My water lines have frozen on and off, even though I leave a slight trickle every night. Water just started flowing yesterday, and I have a steady trickle going in the bathroom. Feels like wasting water, but if it's the only way to keep things flowing... Toilets need to be flushed, dogs need their water, puppies need their water, and of course... I need my bean water, leaf water, and water-water. It's nice to be able to shower too, you know... especially after all that shoveling like an energizer bunny.

I think the roughest part of these past two weeks or so was last Friday, before Saturday's whammy of a bammy-bam storm. My buddy was able to do a Costco run and drive out here with provisions for the dogs and me. Before Friday, for a few days twice daily I was hiking out farther and farther on the road with my snowshoes and the dogs trudging behind. Harley wasn't doing well in this deep snow, even walking on the compacted surface I was leaving behind. The uncompacted, fresh snow was just below or at road sign levels.

One of the nails on Harley's front paw started to get bloody, so I decided to leave them both behind on the hikes. I was able to make a path one mile down the road (it's two miles to the end of the road), and it'd take me about twenty to thirty minutes to just carve out about a quarter mile in fresh powder snow, each step sinking about a foot and half to two feet. You know those stair machines at gyms? Yeah, like that, but at the maximum setting with higher footsteps. That!

So, back to Friday morning. I know it's gonna take my buddy an hour and half, maybe longer, to get here—plus the time he needs to stop by the post office to get my mail and packages. I finally got geared up, and at 10:40 a.m., left the house with a big waterproof backpack. It only took about fifteen to twenty minutes to hike that one mile of path. It took me about fifty minutes to finish the last mile.

If you saw my path, you'd wonder why I didn't take a straight route. I kept trying to stay by the tree lines: due to the branches dumping their snow reserves, the snow underneath would be more packed and compacted—thus less sinking for each step. Doing that did help improve my speed and pace. If I hadn't, it might have taken me twice as long to finish that final mile. I ended up being at the spot earlier than my buddy, and spent the time watching this huge construction machine plowing the snow with plow blades standing maybe eight to ten feet high—that kind of power is what's needed to plow this road, not any regular old pickup truck with a snow blade, as most are used to seeing...

Finally, my buddy arrives, and good news—he brought an older sled for me to put the thirty-five-pound bag of dog food in. I loaded the bag up with all the meats, cheese, milk, etc., and my packages. I would estimate the bag was initially about forty to fifty pounds. To my surprise, he also brought three beers that had been sitting in his garage fridge. He had stopped drinking for some time and gave me those—man, that was the best thing ever! It has been a while since I had beer! We chatted for a bit, caught up on news, and his kid was playing in the snow. Finally, it was time for me to head back—the dogs would be waiting and it was their lunchtime. My buddy took a video of me leaving, with the sled tied to the backpack, as "evidence [I'm] still alive." Ha!

As I started to take off, oof... What the hell did I just get myself into? This extra weight was making me still sink about half a foot or so, even though I was doing my best to step where I had before! It was getting to be harder than I thought I could handle. No, I couldn't let myself think that—this is survival. One step at a time. You can do this, just don't push yourself too hard, take it easy, drink water... (Of course, I filled up a hydration bladder). Twice on the return trip, I took the bag off and unloaded stuff into the sled—the milk alone initially, then the frozen beef and frozen chicken. That made life so much better, but not too much. It took me two hours and fifty minutes to hike the two miles back home, and I still had to let the dogs out and gather more firewood to cut up and split.

Friday was leg day, and Saturday was upper body day. I shoveled nine or ten times, each time a minimum of 5–6" of snow. On Saturday, the snow just kept coming and started to creep up the living room windows. Every day since then, it's been snowing a few inches a day, 'til Wednesday. It started to come down hard again, and I tried my best to keep up with the shoveling—but the toll was hitting my body, and by Thursday morning, I was unable to shovel all the path in one go (steps down, a path straight, two paths to the right, one to the wood shed/log splitter/axe and chopping block, and another to the wood pile). I had to rest and do sections at a time.

I gave up on shoveling Thursday morning and decided to take a few hours off... Okay, yeah, I knew this was a mistake. I'd have to pay the piper, but at the same time, I needed the rest just as badly. Thursday, late afternoon, I tried to shovel, but only did a very small section—it started snowing down in wet granules, which meant each shovelful was even heavier!

I still need to head to the post office and the local store to load up on more provisions. I need fresh fruit and veggies. I currently only have pasta, beef, chicken, bread, milk, and I'm already running low on cheese. Got one can of lentil soup left, and there's a whole bunch of ramen but I have pre-hypertension and need to avoid high-salt products. I got plenty of rice and oatmeal, though that alone will get boring super fast.

I'm running low on dog food too. Damn. Being a mother, Marley eats almost three times more than she normally does! I can't wait until the pups are fully weaned and she's back to her normal diet. But, I've got dog food waiting for me at the post office (Honest Kitchen—honestly, check it out!), as well as puppy training pads. Oh, yeah. I need to dig my car out again. I know if I was on a snowmobile and saw my buried car, I'd have thought it was a huge-ass snow hill and tried to jump it...HA!

Time to catch up with work, school, life, forty-two. Oh yeah, and more shoveling.

TIRED, BUT TRIUMPHANT

By Tammy Willburn Frasier, Preschool Teacher's Assistant and Bus Driver

Yes, the March 2023 snowstorm has been a big one. I hear people saying there has never been snow like this before. Maybe not in their lifetime, or since they moved here, but there has been this much snow several times before.

This time, through experience and a lifetime of preparation, we were able to come through it tired, but triumphant. We were able to keep ourselves plowed out and shoveled out. We were even able to help our neighbors.

Was it hard? Of course! Shoveling and running the tractor for six or seven hours per day is hard on a body.

Was it unusual? For the last few years, yes it was. I personally hope this is a sign that we will start having winter again. Not this much at a time, though! That's for sure.

What I learned was that we are strong, and stronger if we work together as a community. Another thing learned (or remembered) was to keep a positive attitude. When you need to think outside-of-the-box for solving issues without all your usual resources, it makes everything easier if your attitude is right. I personally spent my early mornings as close to normal as I could: coffee and time in prayer and reading my Bible. This keeps me calmer.

The Lord bless you!
Tammy Willburn Frasier

SILENT NIGHT

By Dottie Simmons, Community Member

Silent night,
Cold and muffled by snow,
Glad for those safe at home
By the fire's warm glow.
Worried for those,
Stuck out where they roam,
Cold and hungry,
And maybe alone.
For those on the roads,
All icy and slick,
Wishing they could
Be somewhere else quick.
Nature is beautiful,
But unforgiving.
We follow its lead
To keep on living.
For it's to our detriment,
If we forget,
We're not its boss.
We're just part of it.

LOVELY LANDSCAPES

Photos Submitted By Various Community Members

The snow was treacherous, but gorgeous. The following photos submitted by community members explore the boundless beauty of the natural landscape.

LIKE A CHILD I GO

By Dottie Simmons, Community Member

Like a child I go,
Trudging up in the snow
With my sled,
With a mission quite different from
Sliding instead.
Shades of our early years,
Here in the hills,
In other big storms,
Snowbound and still.
We'd park out by the road,
Before the storm came,
Keep a sled for transporting
Groceries, mail, and more,
When we managed to get out and
Go to the store.
Much older now,
Big storms still come,
And we still get the mail
And still think it is fun.
Though it takes us much longer
And wears us right out,
It's the right life for us,
Without a doubt.

SNOWY BREAK

By Annika Collins, 8th Grade

When the snowstorm started, my parents thought it would be one week long, but it ended up being about two weeks. My parents have a generator, so we had showers and internet throughout the whole time. I'm glad we already had firewood too. If we didn't, then we would have been frozen.

I mostly watched movies and shows the whole time. After a while, I had to go to basketball practice on a Thursday and on Friday a basketball tournament. On Saturday, we went to the award ceremony and they gave us our trophy. They also handed out the all tourneys. Richy, Kaston, and I all got a tourney. After that we went back to the hotel and went to bed. On the way back home the next morning, we went to a beach to take pictures of the team with our basketball tournament trophy.

When I got home, my dog Bella was so excited to see me, and I was happy to be home. I stayed home the rest of the week and watched movies and baked brownies and cookies. And then, sadly, I had to go back to school, and our snow break was done and over with.

FUN SNOW DAYS

By Arielle Yarbrough, 6ᵗʰ Grade

We had a two-week break from school due to a huge amount of snow. I went sledding with my friends and family. It was hard getting up to Mad Rock, but we got up there and had a lot of fun. When I got home, I shoveled the roof and got hot chocolate afterward so that made me happy.

The next day my sister, Evelynne, had a friend come over. They went sledding and then my dad left to go on a control burn. He was gone for twenty days. I went to town and got some turkeys. I had four, but now I only have three. The turkeys are all doing well. I threw snowballs at my dog, and she did a backflip.

The basketball team went to a tournament in Crescent City. After that, we went to Bear River Casino, and I got to play arcade games with Sieanna. At the arcade, I won the Whack-a-Mole and got a thousand points on my game card. I got a gumball machine and then all of us—including me, Sieanna, Colton, Rider, DJ, Wyatt, Lydia, Richy, and Jeremiah—played laser tag. It was kids versus adults. Obviously, the kids ended up winning. After playing laser tag, we ate pizza and Rider had hot wings. After eating we went bowling. The kids had their side, and the adults had the other for some reason. Richy won the bowling match. After that, we went to the movies, and Sieanna and I drank a big blue slushie. It was good. Then me, Sieanna, and my family went to Sea World.

I had a fun time during our snow days, but I was ready to come back to school and see my friends.

THE SNOW NEEDS TO GO AWAY

By Colton Simoes, 7ᵗʰ Grade

During the time we were out of school because of snow, I did a variety of things. First, let's get one thing straight: this SNOW NEEDS TO GO AWAY! It's annoying. All I'm doing is shoveling and getting wet.

During the first couple of days, I was at a basketball tournament in Crescent City. We got second in the tournament (the biggest eighth grade basketball competition).

After that, we helped our neighbor. Then went up Buck Mountain and pulled Kaston and his neighbor out of the snow.

We cut wood about three times, but we are still really low on wood. Also, it was Summer's mom's birthday the weekend before we came back. The snow was mainly only affecting us when we were driving, and that's when I did a lot of shoveling. It did affect Summer because she could not drive her car, and she was stuck at home. Most of the time though, it was just me and my dad at the house with the animals.

Also, during the break we almost ran out of water, so I had to walk up and down, up and down, up and down, and up and down my hill with a water pump. I want this snow to go away. I did not have fun.

IT'S COLD OUTSIDE NOW

By Isaiah Doyle Hackett, 8th Grade

It was very, very, VERY COLD … but alas it was enjoyable. Hot chocolate, brownies, taco soup—magical! I played video games from dawn till dusk and leveled up my characters. I also watched a ton of SpongeBob. When there was no electricity, I slept most of the time. I slept and slept and slept. I did go visit family: my grandma, grandpa, and brother. The snow was around three and a half feet deep. It was a lot, but I had never seen snow, so yeah!

A few times I tried to build an igloo; however, I always got too cold and went back inside. I also made snow cones. They were delish. I had cherry, blueberry, and my favorite: pineapple-coconut. My teeth hurt really bad later because it was cold. I had Halloween Captain Crunch for breakfast every day. Lunch was top ramen and hot dogs. I know it's strange! Dinner was leftovers.

I really, really do not like snow anymore. It was too cold. I froze, and my bones were sore—so very sore, and not to mention, the dog got sprayed by a skunk. At first, I was so excited. I thought it would be amazing: igloos, snowmen, all that, but it was just too cold outside. However, I did find peace with the cold finally when it ended. I was full of relief when the power came back on and we had heat in the house. I was very happy.

THE TWO WEEKS OF SNOW

By Jaden Pacheco, 6ᵗʰ Grade

At the start of the snow week, I played a lot of Monopoly and my mom beat me two times, but I beat her a lot of other times. We had no power due to the storm, but my dad got the generator running so I could play video games. The next day we picked up my friend, Dalan. When we got the power back on, Dalan stayed with us for about a week, then we took him home.

On the way home my mom made a bet with me. If I could make the soft snow into a snowball, then she had to play more Monopoly. I won! When we were playing, the lights turned on and off, and on and off, and on and off–so we unplugged everything and turned off the lights. Since the power was out, we turned on the generator.

Before we did all the fun stuff like playing Monopoly and video games, we had to shovel our driveway and paths for our dogs. Our cat loves the snow. When he walks on it he falls, then he gets back up and attacks it with his paws. He likes to find mice and quail, torture them, and let them go when he gets bored. All week we had to have my dad get wood for us. The two snow weeks seemed to go by fast with all that we did.

SNOW DAYS

By Jerimiah Smith, 8ᵗʰ Grade

During the two weeks that we were out for snow days, I did nothing!!! All I did was sleep and shovel snow and I also had to shovel out my generator that takes gas. And that is all I did during the snow days because I couldn't do anything else. I mean there was nothing else I could do—there was no power and with no power means no microwave or any other food-heating tools, so I played with my Nintendo Switch and just chilled in my house the whole time and when we did get power, I ate noodles. :)

KASTON MELA'S SNOW STORM BREAK

By Kaston Mela, 8th Grade

During my break, I shoveled lots of snow and carried lots of wood inside. There was so much snow that I couldn't really do anything because every time I went outside, I would get really wet or get snow in my boots.

Luckily, this year we didn't really have any trees falling down on the road, so we haven't had to stop and cut any out of the way like past years' winters. Most of the time I was shooting targets and fishing, but when it snowed a lot, I had to just start hanging out inside. Also, when we were at a basketball tournament, I went fishing for a little bit. Well, fishing, the wind was blowing way too hard. The crazy wind even made it hard to cast my line.

On our way back from the tournament, it took us a while because it was raining and also snowing during the drive. Once we were home, we tried to go to the store to get supplies. However, we got stuck in the snow, so we had to dig ourselves out for a while. Before we got ourselves unstuck though, Colton and his dad showed up and helped us get all the way unstuck. They just pulled us right out of the snow, because they have a big Dodge truck. After we got out and finally made it to the store, we bought some snacks. I also went and found some pellets to shoot with my pellet gun and bought some of those. By the time we got home, it was already kinda late, but I didn't really care. So even though it was late, I went outside and set up some soda cans to shoot. After a while of shooting them, I went back inside and hung out.

All I did on my break was shovel snow, carry wood, and shoot targets with my pellet gun, but I had fun and liked not being at school.

AN ICE COLD SNOW BREAK

By Kaydin Myers, 8th Grade

During the break from school, I shoveled a lot of snow and dug out our driveway and in front of our mailbox. I also helped the neighbor shovel his driveway. In the hills of Mad River, California, we get a lot of snow.

The way I keep my house warm is by burning wood in the wood stove. Halfway through the stormy weeks, we ran out of wood. After running out, we had to cut some wood in the snow while it was also raining.

My driveway was full of snow, so I shoveled it out all day. The roads were clear by my house, but some other people were stuck and their houses were snowed-in.

I was out of power, so we had to run our generator for a while. Once we ran out of gasoline for the generator, we went to the store and got some more. We then went home to fuel up the generator.

I also got a compound bow for hunting. Unlike normal bows, compounds use a series of cables and pulleys to provide more force than the flex of the limbs alone. At the same time, those cables and cams create force, which greatly reduces the strength required to hold the bow at full draw, making it easier to take careful aim.

At the end of it all, I was happy but also a little mad because the snow would make for a better summer. On the other hand, the snow was keeping me from doing stuff I needed to do outside, so I was a little happy about the snow altogether.

WEEKS OF MISERY AND SNOW

By Mabel Miranda, 7th Grade

Starting on February 24th, 2023, there was lots of snow, and we had to shovel out our driveway and got stuck numerous times. I shoveled more and more and more snow. I even shoveled snow off of my roof because I saw literal cracks on the inside. After all, there was tons of snow on it.

There wasn't any electricity for a few days, because my generator broke down, so that was not fun. :(Sadly, we had a lack of wood, so we used propane to keep warm and made lots of trips back to Fortuna to get more. My dogs are outside dogs, but don't worry—we set up tarps for them to be warm under, but I still got stressed about if they were fine or not.

I slept a lot because I didn't have much to do except shovel, and it was cold outside. I kept tripping and falling because I had no proper snow shoes. I spent most of my time inside because it was just unbearable outside, repeatedly snowing over and over again nonstop every day. Whenever I woke up to more snow, I wanted it to be summer already.

There was no school for two weeks, and I can't believe I actually missed school after the first week. This whole two weeks was a struggle, and I don't want to go through it again because of how much shoveling I had to do.

We finally went to Redding to see my grandma, and it was nice. Meemaw made us cookies when we came. :) Meemaw has lots of dogs, too. Other than my time with Meemaw, the whole two weeks with no school was not fun. I hate snow now!

WHAT HAPPENED DURING THE SNOW DAYS

By Payton Connor, 6ᵗʰ Grade

It all started on February 22nd with me not going to school because I was sick. I stayed home for two days. It was already super snowy, but on the third day I was awake in my bed reading a book when my mom walked in and told me it was a snow day.

The next day I felt better and we went sledding with my cousin and Arielle's family and some other people. That night Arielle stayed the night at my house. It was pretty fun. For the next couple of days we stayed home. After three days, my cousin left and it started to snow again. Then we went to Colton's house with my family. We hung out, went sledding, and after a while we left and went home.

I don't know exactly how many days after that we went to Crescent City to my brother's basketball tournament. The hotel was also pet-friendly, so we were allowed to bring Kasten's dog, Trout. We couldn't get home because there was too much snow, so I stayed at my cousins' house, and I played VR and swam at a pool. When we got home, there was A LOT of snow. We could barely get up our driveway. I tried to go sledding at my house, but I lost the sled in the snow.

The power being out also made it really dark in my room because I usually have LED lights on, so I lit some candles instead. I put them out before I went to bed. When the power came back on, I played some video games and also watched some TV. One thing disappointed me when the snow started to melt—we had to go back to school.

WORK WORK WORK

By Richard Ferri, 8ᵗʰ Grade

During the two weeks off because of snow, I had to feed every other day and shovel every day. The only friend I got to see during that time, other than at the tournament, was Colt. During the tournament, I hung out with all my friends on the basketball team and a couple friends from other places. On the way back from the tournament, some of us went to the Bear River bowling place. Then the next day I shoveled more snow and fed again. I spent a lot of time with my grandpa and a couple of my cousins. I spent one night with two of my cousins and Colt.

All the nights that my grandma was gone, I cooked for my grandpa. The first day the power went out, we switched all the cords over and turned on the generator. My grandpa and I shoveled a lot of snow, plus we shoveled out dog houses so the dogs could get in easily. My mom couldn't make it out of the house, so I couldn't even go home.

There was enough snow that helicopters came and dropped bales of hay for the cattle where we had leases. I was supposed to get my fair steer soon, but there was too much snow for him to get here. I cut some wood with Colt and some more of my family. I had to run the chain saw because they didn't trust Colt. Colt had to load all the wood, so it was okay because I didn't have to load it.

BORING SNOW DAYS

By Shyann Willburn, 7th Grade

Over the last two weeks at home, all I really did was shovel snow and feed all the animals. We had to fill the animals' water tank with hoses because the water froze in the line connected to the water tank. The only fun thing I did was go to my cousin's house and sled, paint our nails, and stay up all night. The day after it snowed we were going to the store. We made it down the hill fine, but when we were coming home, we got stuck about four times and shoveled a lot.

It took us a few days to make it out to the valley; the first day we had to turn around so that we wouldn't get stuck and not make it back home. I had a snowball fight with my sister, mom, and dad. I hit my dad in the back of the head. Mostly I just stayed in the house and watched movies on my phone. My house had power through the whole snow storm since we have a generator and solar panels. My sister and I had to make many trips outside to get wood for the fire. My dad got a new little dog and watching him run in the deep snow was so funny. In all, it was really boring.

OVER SNOW BREAK

By Sieanna Carter, 7ᵗʰ Grade

Over the time we were out, the snow had a major impact on our lives. It caused us to have power outages and not be able to get out of our driveways. Being stuck at home caused us to not be able to get groceries. But besides that, we had some good and funny times, too, like our dogs trying to walk in the snow; you couldn't even see their legs.

Then there was the time when we went to the Crescent City basketball tournament. We barely got out of the driveway on the way, but we ended up making it in time. We also went to Sea World and got to pet sharks. After the tournament, we went bowling and played arcade games and laser tag. Then we went to the movies and watched Creed 3. It was pretty good. I think there's going to be a fourth Creed movie.

A couple of days after that, my family was waiting for my mom's truck to be fixed so that she could drive to Red Bluff to pick up our new puppy named George. We didn't get to name him because the previous owners already did and he responded to it. He is the cutest little thing ever. We put him on the snow, and he slid. He is such a big baby. He loves being held and never wants to walk!

Lastly, I went to Arielle's where we chilled, did pottery, and went sledding. First, we had to make the track which I did the most of. Then we went down like three times each before we decided to go back inside and get some food, and that was about it for the two weeks off school.

WYATT FRENCH'S BIG SNOW TIME

By Wyatt French, 7ᵗʰ Grade

At the beginning of the snowstorm, the power went out and we had no school. During the storm, I mainly played my Zelda game and sometimes went sledding. We went to town twice for food. My dad got stuck at the beginning of my driveway. To get unstuck, my dad shoveled the snow so he could leave. My dad got power by using our generator. We didn't need to get more gas because we had plenty. I don't know how my dad prepared for the storm, but we never ran out of gas for the generator. He had to cut trees for the fireplace because we ran out of wood. That was my fun snow time.

SNOW, SNOW LET IT SNOW!

By Kimber Allender, 5th Grade

It was very snowy for two weeks and it wasn't fun at all. The second day of snowing, when there was a break in the weather, I had to shovel for hours to make a path around my house just to have it SNOW AGAIN THE VERY NEXT DAY AND FILL IN THE PATH I MADE!!!!!! I WASN'T HAPPY ABOUT THAT AT ALL!!!! :(I also had the morning shift of feeding and my sister had the four o'clock shift. My mom had to shovel out her truck—it took her about two hours to finish digging and the power was out for so long.

Finally, the power came back on the sixth day around four-thirty. I was so happy that I yelled, "The power's on, the power's on!!" at the top pf my lungs. The third day and the fifth day my mom wanted to take a picture of the sunset, but her truck was stuck in the snow, so I volunteered to run down to the post office and take a picture with her phone. I was nearly late, but I got some good pictures. I left at seven fifteen and got home around seven thirty. On the fifth day me and my sister Aleah both walked down to take sunset pictures. Sometime during the two weeks, we went to town, then again, a week later. Then I watched movies most of the time and had to go to school. I was bored half the time—tired, sad, and a little mad at the weather. Just kidding! I was very mad at the weather. I was a little happy about going back to school because I got to interact with people and friends I know.

LOUDEN SPAIN'S STORY

By Louden Spain, Kindergarten

I didn't like being out of school for two weeks. I got tired of waiting. While I was off of schoo , I helped my dad cut wood.

I got stuck in the dog trail. As I was walking on the trail, I sunk in up to my chest! I had to dig myself out. Another time I jumped off a metal gate and sunk up to my knees. My mom helped me that time.

There was so much snow I was able to snowboard right at my house. My dad drove the buggy up the hill, and I was able to snowboard down his tracks. That was fun!

Thankfully, we have a generator, so the power outage was not that big of a deal. We did get some new leaks in the roof. I put my toy helmets under them to catch the water.

All in all, I am happy to be back in school.

FUN, BUT NOT FUN

By Levi Cheney, 4th Grade

Shoveling this snow is a challenging task that I have to do because I am small and the snow is heavy. Feeding the dogs and cats is another task of mine. It is fun to be inside and play with my toys and games. On March 9, 2023, I was outside for five hours shoveling, getting firewood, and house-fixing. Our firewood shed was about to collapse. They put new supports to keep it up. March 11, 2023, we ran out of firewood! Thankfully we had one more type of firewood. I am sick of the snow. I thought about when there will be no more snow. I played video games to pass some of the time.

We are not prepared for this winter! We have four feet of snow! The snow was fun because there was no school. The snow was not fun because we had to deal with four feet of snow! But I am delighted to see my friends again. Some snow blocked our door when it fell off the roof. There was so much of it. I am going to be so happy when the snow is gone. I sank into the snow up to my chest when I jumped off the roof! I couldn't even go sledding! All in all, I am glad we are back in school.

STUCK AT HOME

By Oscar Liufau, 5th Grade

I have been stuck at home for three weeks, but it wasn't that bad. My mom made biscuits and I jumped off the roof. The snow is up to my chest!. I wasn't able to sled because my sled was buried in the snow.

A bad part was running out of propane and the power going out, and the worst part was the snow burying our wood. Cash got some wood rounds out of the snow, thankfully. Some of the fun parts was seeing a skunk and having snowball fights with my brother, Cash.

IT WAS A GOOD TWO WEEKS OF SNOW!

By Charlie Stewart, 2nd Grade

At the beginning of the snowstorm, the power went out and we had no school. During the storm, I mainly played my Zelda game and sometimes went sledding. We went to town twice for food. My dad got stuck at the beginning of my driveway. To get unstuck, my dad shoveled the snow so he could leave. My dad got power by using our generator. We didn't need to get more gas because we had plenty. I don't know how my dad prepared for the storm, but we never ran out of gas for the generator. He had to cut trees for the fireplace because we ran out of wood. That was my fun snow time.

US

Photos Submitted By Various Community Members

Community members had to pull together to make it through, while finding the mental and emotional space to somehow enjoy the snow. The following photos submitted by locals illuminate the sense of camaraderie and joy that also marked the era.

AFTERWORD

By Ama Karikari-Yawson, Editor and Publisher

"In the depth of winter, I finally learned that within me there lay an invincible summer."
- Albert Camus

This is my third time partnering with Southern Trinity JUSD on a book project, and as always, it has been such a privilege and immense honor. Their photos and reflections evoke a wave of different feelings, such as sadness, frustration, and anger—as well as joy, humor, and awe.

This book provides many lessons regarding disaster preparedness and disaster survival. Unfortunately, many scientists believe that such catastrophes may become the new normal. In its 2021 report, the Intergovernmental Panel on Climate Change (IPCC) forewarned that human activity is changing the climate in unprecedented—and perhaps irreversible—ways, and that the world has already experienced horrifying, extreme weather caused by climate change, record temperatures, and rapid ice melt.[1]

If we do not engage in drastic action to reduce carbon emissions, more and more merciless weather patterns may be on the horizon. That said, the Southern Trinity JUSD community has engaged in a great act in creating this book. On a personal level, writing reflections has certainly helped the contributors process their trauma. On a community level, a valuable record has been created for posterity. But, on a global level, they have shown the world about the struggles caused by natural disasters and have thereby created their own plea for positive climate action. There are blessings ahead for the Southern Trinity JUSD community.

---

1   https://www.bbc.com/future/article/20230317-the-state-of-the-climate-in-2023

THE PEOPLE WHO MADE THIS POSSIBLE

Peggy Canale, Superintendent, Principal, and Teacher

Peggy Canale is a native of Southern Trinity County and attended STJUSD for grades K–12. Upon graduation, she attended College of the Redwoods, then transferred to Chico State University where she acquired a BA in Social Welfare. After working for the Tehama County Department of Welfare, she married and returned to Southern Trinity in 1983. Ms. Canale began teaching at Hoaglin-Zenia in 1985, where she taught for eight years. She transferred to Van Duzen Elementary in 1993 and taught full time until 2006. Upon receiving her administrative credential through Simpson College in Redding, she worked as a teacher/vice principal for several years before taking on the role of Superintendent/Principal in 2006. Ms. Canale has worked in this role for the past 17 years. Most recently, was chosen as the Region 1 ACSA (Association of California School Administrators) Superintendent of the Year.

In 2021, she passed her principal duties on to Andrew Felt, and has transitioned back into the classroom at Hoaglin-Zenia in the role of superintendent/teacher.

Ama Karikari-Yawson, Milestales Founder and President

Ms. Yawson earned a BA in Social Studies (cum laude) from Harvard University, an MBA from the Wharton School, and a JD from the University of Pennsylvania Law School.

Her unique understanding of social issues, business, and the law has enabled her to become a relevant voice on issues as varied as race relations, women's issues, dating, parenting, self-love, hair bullying, and entrepreneurship. Her articles have been published in MSNBC's *The Grio, The Huffington Post, The Atlantic, Madame Noire,* and other publications. Ms. Yawson has also appeared on *The Today Show,* Al Jazeera's *The Stream, The Nate Berkus Show,* and Fox Business.

In 2013, a painful experience—during which a barber called her son a racial pejorative term and said that his hair was not pretty and should be shaved off—inspired Ms. Yawson to venture into writing empowering children's books. Her first book, *Sunne's Gift,* provides the universal message of self-love and being true to one's own gifts and passions. She was so touched by the story that she quit her job as senior counsel at Citigroup, Inc. to start her own publishing and education company, Milestales.

Through Milestales, Ms. Yawson and her partners provide books, performances, enrichment programs, and training sessions to corporations, schools, libraries, churches, prisons, institutes, and other organizations.

Ms. Yawson currently lives in New York City with her husband and two elementary-school-aged sons.

COMMUNITY CONTRIBUTORS

Contributors - Van Duzen Elementary Students

Annika Collins - Grade 8
Arielle Yarbrough - Grade 6
Colton Simoes - Grade 7
Isaiah Doyle Hackett - Grade 8
Jaden Pacheco - Grade 6
Jerimiah Smith - Grade 8
Kaston Mela - Grade 8
Kaydin Myers - Grade 8
Mabel Miranda - Grade 7
Payton Connor - Grade 6
Richard Ferri - Grade 8
Shyann Willburn - Grade 7
Sieanna Carter - Grade 7
Wyatt French - Grade 7

Contributors - Hoaglin-Zenia Elementary Students

Charlie Stewart - Grade 2
Kimber Allender - Grade 5
Levi Cheney - Grade 4
Louden Spain - Kindergarten
Oscar Liufau - Grade 5

Community Contributors - Adults

Ali Matheson – Teacher
Andrew Felt - Principal
Caitlin Canale - Preschool Teacher and Ruth Lake Community Service District Manager
Dottie Simmons - Community Member
Jesse Ragsdale - Community Member
Ken Richardson - Community Member
Pam Peace - Community Member
Peggy Canale - Superintendent, Principal, and Teacher
Suzy Hall – Teacher
Susie Toerpe – Teacher
Tammy Willburn Frasier - Preschool Teacher's Assistant/Bus Driver
Terri Willburn - Assistant at Hoaglin-Zenia Elementary

Article copied with Permission.

Matt LaFever - Mendocino County Educator and Journalist
Kym Kemp - Journalist, Photographer, and Entrepreneur

THE INSTITUTIONS THAT MADE THIS POSSIBLE

SOUTHERN TRINITY JOINT UNIFIED SCHOOL DISTRICT

Southern Trinity Joint Unified School District is committed to providing excellence in educational programs for each student's achievement and success.

Guided by the highest expectations, STJUSD provides our students with a broad range of rigorous educational opportunities. Staff enable students to reach their full potential and successfully meet the demands and opportunities of a highly technological twenty-first century.

Students graduate with core knowledge and skills that become the building blocks for lifelong learning. They advance forward with a positive attitude and the leadership, character, and academic skills necessary to excel in a global arena.

Families are an integral part of the educational process. In recognition of this important role, family involvement is actively sought, encouraged, and welcomed.

Business and community partnerships greatly enhance our students' learning experiences and educational opportunities, offering them opportunities to apply their learning to real-world situations.

Schools serve as community hubs, places where the community gathers to celebrate and improve learning through the enjoyment of art, music, sports, public speaking, drama, and other school-related activities. The use of school facilities by the community is encouraged.

School facilities are a reflection of the entire community. We provide students with the educational tools to meet the technological demands of the future, and the social skills to function in a culturally diverse society.

MILESTALES

Milestales is a publishing, media, and education consulting firm that strives to provide stories that help us to grow emotionally, physically, and mentally—so that we can achieve our greatest dreams, both individually and collectively. Milestales achieves this aim by producing socially conscious and culturally aware books and media.

Additionally, Milestales provides training sessions, workshops, performances, arts residencies, and enrichment programs to schools, universities, organizations, and corporations.

Through its network of artists, educators, academics, and thought leaders, Milestales services a number of clients including the New York City Department of Education, State University of New York, GEAR UP at Nassau Community College, Nassau BOCES, Eastern Suffolk BOCES, and other school districts, organizations, and corporations.

Arts and enrichment programs offered include storytelling, publishing, college and career readiness, entrepreneurship, vocal music, meditation, chess, African djembe drumming, and STEM. Training sessions surround diversity and inclusion, social and emotional learning, respect for all (bullying prevention), sexual autonomy (sexual violence prevention), culturally responsive education, supporting students with special needs, mindfulness, and much more. Moreover, Milestales offers a number of storytelling and musical performances by New York's top talent.

Email: info@milestales.com
Phone: 347-886-2026
Website: www.milestales.com

www.milestales.com